God's Way to Keep a Church Going & Growing

Vergil Gerber

God's Way to Keep a Church Going & Growing

William Carey Library
South Pasadena, California

A Division of G/L Publications
Glendale, California, U.S.A.

Co-published by
Regal Books Division, G/L Publications
Glendale, California 91209
and William Carey Library
South Pasadena, California 91030

Library of Congress Catalog No. 73-944-11
ISBN 0-8307-0294-6

CONTENTS

Introduction: Donald A. McGavran   7

Why This Manual?   9

SECTION I   **BIBLICAL BEDROCK
FOR EVANGELISM/CHURCH GROWTH**   11

     1   *The Evangelistic Goal*   13

     2   *The Spiritual Dynamic*   19

     3   *Scriptural Strategy*   23

SECTION II   **AN EXPERIMENT
IN EVALUATING EVANGELISM**   29

SECTION III   **AIDS FOR DIAGNOSING
YOUR EVANGELISTIC PROGRAM**   43

SECTION IV   **A PERSONAL WORKBOOK FOR
EVALUATING EVANGELISTIC
EFFECTIVENESS**   71

INTRODUCTION

This manual by Dr. Gerber fills an urgent need. Conscience on evangelism and church growth has been mounting for several years. Information about effective evangelism has been piling up in books and magazines. Church growth seminars and workshops are burgeoning in many lands. Leaders seek to communicate information about evangelistic methods which God has blessed to Christians operating at the grass roots. In evangelism, victory is won in local churches or is not won at all. Believers are built into The Body only when they become responsible members of on going congregations.

But precisely at the grass roots we have lacked a manual which would help work-a-day pastors and missionaries evaluate their evangelistic programs, recognize the doors God is opening before them, and achieve effectiveness in winning men to Christ and multiplying churches.

This *Manual for Evangelism/Church Growth* may mark the beginning of a new era in evangelism at home and abroad. Simply by using it as guide (and enriching his own mind with the stimulating supplementary reading at the end of each chapter) the pastor/missionary can conduct a three day workshop in church planting evangelism. In English speaking groups a copy for each member should be obtained. For groups speaking other languages, this book should be translated and published locally. Till that happens, if the leader knows English, he can use the book to good effect for many of its techniques are independent of language.

In short, this manual will help ministers and missionaries at home and abroad lead Christians to focus on biblical goals and pierce through the fog of good intentions and rosy estimates to the actual situation. We always gain by seeing reality. From there, we can discern the real possibilities for church growth.

I commend the book and trust it will soon be translated into the major languages of earth and used to train hundreds of thousands of leaders in beginning principles of effective evangelism and church growth.

January, 1973

Donald McGavran
School of Missions and
Institute of Church Growth
Fuller Theological Seminary
Pasadena, California

WHY THIS MANUAL?

The need for some kind of vehicle for encouraging and developing core studies, experimentation, and how-to-go-about-it aids in evangelism/church growth became evident several years ago when 50 IFMA/EFMA mission executives with work in Latin America met to discuss the 421-page *CGRILA* report prepared by Read, Monterroso and Johnson and published under the title *LATIN AMERICAN CHURCH GROWTH.* The gathering, known as the Elburn Consultation and held in Elburn, Illinois, in September, 1970, recognized the dearth of hard facts and figures to build upon.

The need was magnified significantly in the next several years as requests for assistance began to come in from church and mission leaders in many countries.

The objectives for preparing this manual are to provide:
1. Minimum biblical core studies in evangelism/church growth.
2. Basic materials for meaningful participation in evangelism/church growth workshops.
3. Practical aids for diagnostic research.
4. Encouragement and assistance in continuing evaluation, experimentation and studies in evangelism/church growth.

Even before the basic English text was completed, work began on translations into Spanish, German and Norwegian. And it is anticipated that the manual will be available in numerous other languages and used widely around the world as a:

1. Textbook for evangelism/church growth workshops.
2. Tool for self-evaluation of past and present evangelistic efforts.
3. Guide for setting evangelistic goals and planning evangelistic strategy.
4. System for developing continuing evaluation of evangelistic efforts.
5. Stimulus for encouraging fruitful evangelism throughout the world.

The manual can be used equally well in relation to a local church, group of churches or a whole denomination.

ACKNOWLEDGEMENTS:

I am deeply indebted to a number of colleagues for their invaluable assistance and counsel in preparing this manual. Especially to those who worked so closely with me in the final preparations and draft. They include: C. Peter Wagner, Donald McGavran, Arthur F. Glasser, Ralph D. Winter. Special appreciation also to Jean Mueller and Doris Wagner who gave of themselves and their secretarial skills "beyond the call of duty."   *V.G.*

SECTION I

BIBLICAL BEDROCK
FOR
EVANGELISM /
CHURCH GROWTH

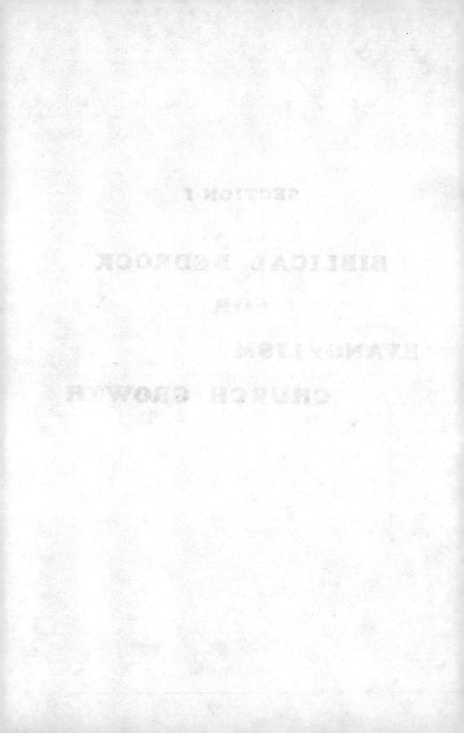

THE EVANGELISTIC GOAL

The Biblical goal of evangelism is given to us in Matthew 16:18. The Lord Jesus Himself said:

> "I will build *MY CHURCH;*
> and the gates of Hell shall
> not prevail against it."

When He commissioned His disciples to carry out their evangelistic task, once again the church was at the heart of His command:

> "Going into all the world
> you are to *MAKE DISCI-
> PLES* of all nations, baptiz-
> ing them in the name of the
> Father, and of the Son, and
> of the Holy Spirit: teaching
> them to observe all things
> which I have commanded
> you."
>
> Matthew 28:19-20

The central imperative of The Great Commission is to *MAKE DISCIPLES*. This means bringing men and women to Jesus Christ so that they give Him the all-inclusive "yes" of submission and faith.

All the other action words in these verses are helping verbs. They are "going", "baptizing" and "teaching."

It is a continuous process by which men who are converted to Jesus Christ relate themselves to each other and become responsible, reproducing church members. These disciples go out to make other disciples, baptizing, teaching, and relating them to the church also.

The evangelistic task, therefore, falls short of its objective unless it relates new converts to local congregations of believers.

On the Day of Pentecost the First Church in Jerusalem made up of 120 members added 3,000 to its fellowship in one day. These in turn reached out into the urban community around them gaining favor with people. And day after day the Lord added to their number people who were being saved. It was a continuous process ("being saved") in which the church became both the goal and the agent of dynamic evangelism.

Acts 2:41-47

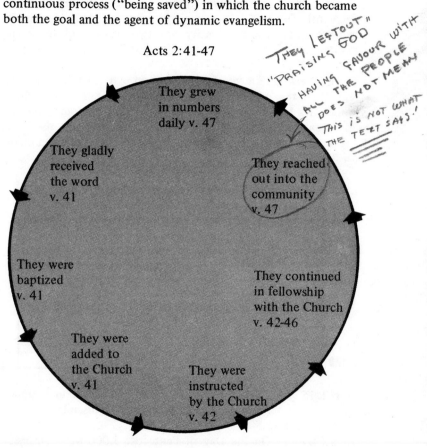

In the New Testament evangelistic effectiveness is a quality that is constantly measured in quantitative terms. Precise figures are given regarding the number of professions of faith (quantity). These are always based upon those who follow on, are baptized and continue in the Apostles' doctrine, fellowship, breaking of bread, and prayers (quality). Just as faith without works is dead, so spiritual growth in the New Testament is frequently expressed in terms of quantities. This is possible because quality and quantity are two aspects of the same reality.

The New Testament gives us a thorough, well-documented report on the origins and growth of First Century churches. Sometimes it is easier to "spiritualize" such a report than to document the conclusions with hard statistics. But the New Testament report is carefully documented with precise numerical figures: *But is STRANGELY SILENT ABOUT SPECIFIC "ACTIVITIES" OF "OUTREACH"*

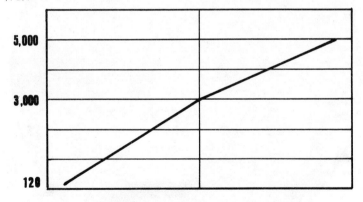

Acts 1:15   The First Church in Jerusalem began in an upper room with a small band of 120 disciples.

Acts 2:41-42   On the Day of Pentecost 3,000 were baptized, instructed in the Word, and added to the Jerusalem community (Koinonia).

Acts 4:4   With careful detail Dr. Luke records the growth pattern from the Day of Pentecost to the imprisonment and questioning of the early disciples. The membership of the Jerusalem church now stands at 5,000.

Acts 5:14   Here the emphasis is upon the fact that *multitudes* of men and women were added.

Acts 6:1, 7   This time the number of disciples was *multiplied*.

From this point on both the Book of Acts and the New Testament Epistles underscore the *multiplication of churches* as well as church members. New congregations were planted in every pagan center of the then-known world in less than four decades.

NOT CITED

Acts 9:31   Church multiplication here is not in terms of a single church, i.e. the First Church of Jerusalem, but in the collective sense of geographical multiplication of believers in all Judea, and Galilee and Samaria. It focuses on the transition from the mother church to emerging congregations in other places.

Acts 16:5   Here again is the change from church (singular) to churches (plural). *Churches* were planted. *Churches* increased in number daily. The Great Commission cannot be divorced from visible, structured, organized churches. In order to function and fulfill the Great Commission, there has to be some kind of structure.

Acts 21:20   Paul uses the word "myriads" in his report. A myriad is a measurement of 10,000. So the apostle reports tens of thousands of Jews alone who turned to Christ and became identified with local churches.

THE ULTIMATE EVANGELISTIC GOAL

Thus evangelism in the New Testament does not stop with
reaching people with the Gospel
nor with the proclamation of the Gospel
nor with public professions of faith in the Gospel
nor even with relating them to the church through baptism
and teaching.

The evangelistic goal is not fulfilled until these new converts
become reproducing Christians who complete the cycle and
guarantee the continuous process of evangelism/church growth.
The ultimate evangelistic goal in the New Testament, therefore,
is two-fold:

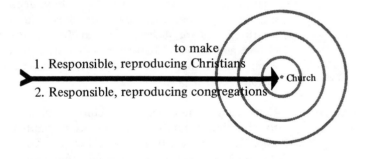

to make
1. Responsible, reproducing Christians
2. Responsible, reproducing congregations

Church

For further reading:

Donald McGavran, "God's Will and Church Growth," in *Understanding
Church Growth* (Grand Rapids, Eerdmans, 1970), pp. 31-48.
C. Peter Wagner, "Evangelism and Saturation Evangelism" in *Frontiers in
Missionary Strategy* (Chicago, Moody Press, 1971), pp. 122-138.
Alan R. Tippett, "Church Growth as a Biblical Concept," in *Church
Growth and the Word of God* (Grand Rapids, Eerdmans, 1970), pp.
9-27.
Ralph D. Winter, "Quality or Quantity?" in *Crucial Issues in Missions
Tomorrow* (Chicago, Moody Press, 1972), pp. 175-187.

THE SPIRITUAL DYNAMIC

Evangelism and church growth are the work of the Holy Spirit. Numerical addition and multiplication can never be substituted for the spiritual reproduction of new life through the Holy Spirit. He is the life of the believer and in turn the life of the Church. There is no evangelism and no church growth apart from Him. He is the spiritual dynamic producing both the quality and the quantity in true New Testament evangelism and church growth.

Luke 24:45-49

v. 45-47   The evangelistic *MESSAGE* of repentance and forgiveness through the suffering and resurrection of Christ is based upon Holy Scripture.

v. 47   The evangelistic *MANDATE* is to share this message with all nations.

v. 48   The evangelistic *METHOD* is through human witnesses (men).

v. 49   The evangelistic *MEANS* is the dynamic of the Holy Spirit.

One hundred twenty *disciples,* men and women fully committed to the evangelistic goal and in absolute obedience to their Lord's command, were told to wait in the upper room until the *MEANS* was provided for them to fulfill their task (v. 49). So they did. The result:

Acts 2

On the Day of Pentecost when the Holy Spirit was given to the waiting disciples, we see a responsible church growing out of their witness.

v. 4   Filled with the Holy Spirit these first disciples began to witness.

v. 5   Men from every nation of the then-known world were on hand in Jerusalem and heard their witness.

v. 6-11   The proclamation of the message was not unintelligible to their multi-lingual audience. It was effective communication resulting in 3,000 professions, baptisms, and additions to the Jerusalem "koinonia." As they heard and received the witness in their own tongue, in turn they carried the spiritual seeds of the church back with them to their native soil.

Result:

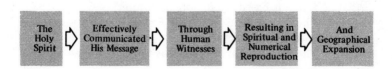

The Holy Spirit ⇨ Effectively Communicated His Message ⇨ Through Human Witnesses ⇨ Resulting in Spiritual and Numerical Reproduction ⇨ And Geographical Expansion

What is significant to us is that from the very beginning a clear organizational structure emerges among the Jerusalem community with all the characteristics of a responsible church.

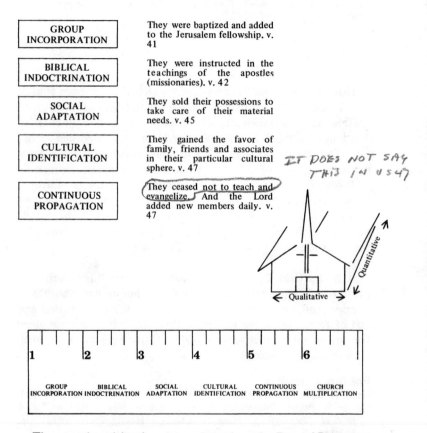

GROUP INCORPORATION	They were baptized and added to the Jerusalem fellowship. v. 41
BIBLICAL INDOCTRINATION	They were instructed in the teachings of the apostles (missionaries). v. 42
SOCIAL ADAPTATION	They sold their possessions to take care of their material needs. v. 45
CULTURAL IDENTIFICATION	They gained the favor of family, friends and associates in their particular cultural sphere. v. 47
CONTINUOUS PROPAGATION	They ceased not to teach and evangelize. And the Lord added new members daily. v. 47

IT DOES NOT SAY THIS IN v 47

1	2	3	4	5	6
GROUP INCORPORATION	BIBLICAL INDOCTRINATION	SOCIAL ADAPTATION	CULTURAL IDENTIFICATION	CONTINUOUS PROPAGATION	CHURCH MULTIPLICATION

The atomic spiritual energy released on the Day of Pentecost set off a chain reaction which shook the world of the first century. This dynamic quality in the person of the Holy Spirit is given for the precise purpose of multiplying nuclear spiritual cells (churches) throughout the world.

Acts 1:8

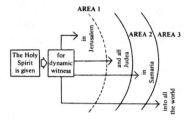

This new Spiritual dynamic empowered the newborn church with a supernatural quality enabling her to fulfill her God-given mission of evangelism/church growth. It is this *qualitative* dimension coupled to the *quantitative* growth recorded in the New Testament which gives breadth and depth to the evangelistic mandate. From the Day of Pentecost on dynamic, living cells multiply into hundreds of congregations in Asia, Europe, Africa, and around the world. The Book of Acts is the opening chapter of the records of church history. It records the details of first century church multiplication through evangelistic witness and in the power of the Holy Spirit.

It is the Holy Spirit who brought the church into being on the Day of Pentecost and who launched her on her evangelistic course. And our interpretation of Acts 2 will be distorted and out of focus unless we recognize that the Holy Spirit was given for the specific purpose of enabling Christ's disciples to fulfill their evangelistic role.

For further reading:

Harry R. Boer, *Pentecost and Missions,* (Grand Rapids, Eerdmans, 1961).

George W. Peters, "Missionary Theology and the New Testament," in *A Biblical Theology of Missions* (Chicago, Moody Press, 1972), pp. 131-156.

Melvin L. Hodges, "Creating Climate for Church Growth," in *Church Growth and Christian Mission* (New York, Harper & Row, 1965), pp. 27-39.

R. Calvin Guy, "Theological Foundations," in *Church Growth and Christian Mission* (New York, Harper & Row, 1965), pp. 40-56.

SCRIPTURAL STRATEGY

"Making disciples" involves *people*. Responsible, reproducing Christians are *people* who are committed to Christ and to His command to make other *people* disciples too, and to relate them to communities of Christian *people* called churches.

Churches are *people*. Responsible, reproducing churches are communities of *people* who are committed to Christ and to His command to establish other communities of Christian *people*.

People are both the object of the evangelistic goal and the agent of evangelistic strategy in the Scriptures. Jesus realized how important strategy is. Since *people* are His method for achieving His evangelistic goal, Jesus gave His disciples several parables having to do with strategy by which they could measure their success or failure.

THE PARABLE OF THE TALENTS (Matt. 25)

"Goal setting" for the disciples of Jesus' time would probably have been a strange term. So Jesus talks to them about their spiritual gifts in terms of "financial investments" rather than goal setting.

Every disciple, He implies, has been given one or another of these gifts to achieve the evangelistic goal. Every disciple is expected to "invest" his gift or gifts in a way that will bring maximum, measurable results in terms of that goal. How the investment is made (strategy) will determine how great or how small the results will be. These results can be objectively and statistically measured. What Jesus is saying is that disciples must become responsible, reproducing Christians.

The word "responsible" is qualitative as well as quantitative. It makes *people* responsible for Christian worship, leadership, education, service, finances, and evangelistic outreach. These qualities of church life can all be measured quantitatively because they involve *people. People* are countable. And *people* can be counted on. Therefore their evangelistic effectiveness is not measured subjectively but objectively. When responsibilities (the use of gifts) are fulfilled, the results can be accurately determined. Success or failure to a large degree will depend on strategy.

A responsible church is made up of *people* who are *responsible* for

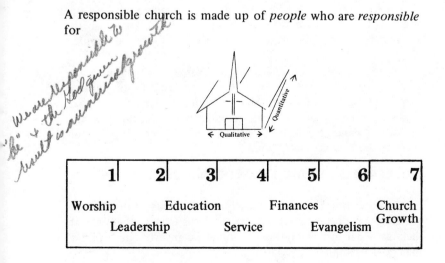

A word of *caution:* Expansion of membership rolls is not the only criterion of success. There are, of course, highly resistant peoples where growth in membership is very difficult. But the use of precise figures in the New Testament is at least *one* way our Lord has given by which we can know whether we are succeeding of failing. And whether our methods are right or whether they need to be changed.

THE PARABLE OF THE SOILS (Matt. 13:1-23)

Usually we call this the parable of the sower, but the intent of the parable concentrates on the soils rather than on the sower. Some soils are more productive than others. Here there are four types of soil. Three are resistant. One is responsive.

Obviously Jesus is not conveying the idea that we should sow seed in every direction. Quite the contrary. The very fact that He points out these different soils is to prepare us for discerning the varying degrees of responsiveness which we can expect even under similar circumstances and to intelligently develop our strategy with the specific goal of obtaining fruit.

Some of the obvious lessons are:
1. Sow with a definite goal in view of reaping fruit.
2. Sowing seed is not the final goal. It is not an end in itself.
3. Where the seed is sown is of vital importance in terms of results.
4. Reaping fruit will depend on responsive soil.
5. Spreading the seed on resistant soils will bring little or no results.
6. Soils need to be pre-tested to determine their responsiveness or resistance.
7. Intelligent sowing is a prerequisite to abundant harvest.
8. Soil is considered high *quality* because of its ability to produce a high *quantity* of fruit. Quality is the measurement of quantity and quantity a measurement of quality.

A word of caution: Methods and strategy, though highly important, are not productive under all conditions. Sometimes a long period of time is needed before the seed germinates. Sometimes the soil is non-responsive for other reasons. We do not have a "fool proof" soil tester to guarantee the degree of responsiveness of all soils. Even the very definition of responsiveness varies greatly in evangelical circles.

But the parable of the soils does make clear that we are to have measurable goals in view, i.e. fruit. And that we are to do all we can to pre-test the soils in determining our strategy.

THE PARABLE OF THE HARVEST (Matt. 9:37-38)

The first and most obvious lesson to be learned from the parable is that the harvest is dead ripe and therefore the need for laborers is critical. But the "dead-ripe" harvest also points up:

1.   Abundant fruit is the end goal of evangelism.

We are not to be primarily concerned with landscaping, fence building, even cultivating and pruning. Right now, the only thing that matters is picking the fruit that is ripe. Fruit is a measurable objective. Whether we pick in terms of bushels or by ones and twos depends on our end goal. Jesus said:

"Herein is my Father glorified
that ye bear *much* fruit;
So shall ye be my disciples."
John 15:8

2.   Pick the fruit when it is ripe.

Timing is very important in Spriptural strategy. We must pick the fruit *when* it is ripe. Or we lose it. If we do not reach rural peoples who move into the big awesome urban centers of our world right at the time when they arrive and are searching for meaningful reality, six months hence the fruit may have fallen to the ground never to be reaped or salvaged.

3. We must go where the fruit is.

There are unbelievable numbers of responsive areas throughout the world that are truly "ripe unto harvest" today. But the laborers are few. While it is also true that there are many resistant areas where the fruit is still green and needs to be cared for and prepared for later harvest, we dare not concentrate the major part of our evangelistic resources on such areas where little or no fruit can be expected while dead ripe fruit hangs in abundance on responsive vines elsewhere. The redeployment of personnel and resources where tangible, measurable results are assured demands our first priority. And a prayerful preparation ("Pray ye the Lord of the Harvest!") is the Scriptural means to determining a fruitful strategy.

For further reading:

C. Peter Wagner, "Why a Missionary Strategy?" and "Biblical Principles for a Strategy of Missions," in *Frontiers in Missionary Strategy* (Chicago, Moody Press, 1971), pp. 15-47.

Donald McGavran, "Today's Task, Opportunity, and Imperative in Missions," in *Understanding Church Growth* (Grand Rapids, Eerdmans, 1970), pp. 49-63.

Alan R. Tippett, "The Holy Spirit and Responsive Populations," in *Crucial Issues in Missions Tomorrow* (Chicago, Moody Press, 1972) pp. 77-101.

Arthur F. Glasser, "Confession, Church Growth, and Authentic Unity in Missionary Strategy," in *Protestant Crosscurrents in Mission,* (Nashville, Abingdon, 1968), pp. 178-222.

SECTION II

AN EXPERIMENT
IN EVALUATING
EVANGELISM

AN EXPERIMENT IN EVALUATING EVANGELISM

At the invitation of the President of the United Evangelical Convention of Venezuela, in March of 1972, C. Peter Wagner and I met with church and mission leaders in the cities of Caracas and Maracaibo. Although most of the leaders present were related to the national convention, other evangelical groups were also represented and invited to participate at the ground level of the ad-hoc discussions.

Their concern was two-fold:
1. How do we evaluate the effectiveness of the evangelistic efforts carried out by our respective groups and denominations?
2. How do we conserve the results and achieve permanence in terms of the church and its growth?

Participants expressed deep concern that extensive evangelistic campaigns have been carried out by all of their groups in the past with evident success in terms of professions of faith. Yet looking back upon them a few years later, the same statistical success is not always reflected either in church membership rolls or in new congregations. This disturbed them.

The result: A 3-year pilot experiment was launched to help meet this two-fold need.

The second week of June of the same year, 47 pastors, leaders, and missionaries gathered at the Evangelical Free Church campgrounds in El Limon for the first of a series of three workshops to be held at one year intervals. Between workshops measurable evangelistic goals projected by each individual group during the four days of intensive study and interchange were to be carried out with careful documentation of details and results for review at the next year's workshop.

The participants represented 72 local churches from 7 different denominations. They came highly motivated. They wanted help in analyzing their churches accurately. They wanted to increase their fruitfulness as God's harvesters. They realized that this was only a pilot project — an experiment-in-depth — but they felt after much thought and prayer that the program projected would at least give them something measurable by which continuing evaluation of their efforts might be possible. They realized that spiritual renewal was basic to the success of the program and they waited upon God for the results.

But they also realized their need for outside technical assistance from qualified resource personnel. Turning to the Evangelical Committee on Latin America (EFMA/IFMA) for assistance, they were provided a resource team of three men to conduct the experiment:

* C. Peter Wagner of the Fuller Evangelistic Association and the Institute of Church Growth in Pasadena, California.
* Edward Murphy, experienced missionary and Director for Latin-America of Overseas Crusades.
* Ruperto Velez, Colombian pastor, evangelist and the Crusades' field director for Colombia.

The project was organized and directed entirely by leaders in Venezuela. Organization, of course, was minimal. Since it was a "first" of its kind, there was no preparatory manual available. No preliminary research was assigned to enhance the value of the first workshop. The time factor did not allow for meaningful reading prior to the gathering. But the growing enthusiasm throughout the four days and the spontaneous expressions of committment at the conclusion to better methods and more daring goals indicated that something important had happened.

The experiment involved five distinct *PHASES*, each of which was allowed a certain flexibility as to time for development.

CYCLE ONE

The June 1972 workshop represented the *FIRST CYCLE* of what has now come to be known as "The Venezuelan Experiment." The curriculum for the first workshop involved four distinct *PHASES*, each of which was allowed a certain flexibility as to time for development.

Curriculum

PHASE I Emphasis upon the Spiritual dynamic of evangelism in church growth was foundational to everything else. Ruperto Velez provided the core of spiritual and biblical insights. This was followed by principles of evangelism/church growth theory. The biblical and theological bases, goal setting as a basis for strategy, research techniques in the use of statistics and graphs, and local case studies were the major ingredients of the curriculum.

PHASE II The participants were then divided into homogeneous groups of four to five. They talked together about their areas, analyzing them on the basis of what they learned in Phase I. Each group was asked to identify some method which God is blessing or some particular fertile field. A spokesman for each group was asked to report briefly to the plenary session with opportunity for discussion after the report. The objective was to cross-fertilize ideas and stimulate thinking growing out of their actual experiences, rather than to follow carefully prepared programs exported from abroad.

PHASE III   In the plenary session which followed graph paper was distributed and each person was taught step-by-step how to plot the membership of his church over the last decade. The name of each participant, the name and location of his church, and statistics related to his work were recorded in a central place. Then each one plotted with a dotted line the biological growth over the same decade (25% per decade was used as a rule of thumb). After which they plotted the biological growth for the next *four years.*

Once again they broke up into small groups and each person carefully and prayerfully asked God how much fruit he can expect in his church over these next four years. The biological growth point obviously was a minimum. Stress was also given to the need for growing through multiplying *churches.* They talked about the challenge of the mother-daughter church concept. Each one then projected by faith the planting of daughter churches and estimated their membership over the same four years. These projections were discussed and approved in the small groups before being finalized.

The next step was a dramatic "faith promise" experiment. Back in plenary session, comments were encouraged. There was plenty of room for discussion at each point. Participants were encouraged to challenge each other. Each report recorded membership, number of daughter churches, and daughter church membership. When all the reports were in, they were added up and the statistics and projections summarized according to the following model:

	PAST				PROJECTED		
	1961	1971	Numerical Increase 1961-71	% Decade Increase 1961-71	1975	4-year Projected Increase	% Decadal Increase 1971-75
TOTAL CHURCHES	23	72	48	200%	130	58	200%
TOTAL MEMBERS	1,975	3,457	1,482	75%	6,655	3,198	215%
44 Churches Represented by Pastors	1,315	1,989	674	50%	3,566	1,577	198%
46 Projected Daughter Churches					1,038		
TOTALS					4,604	2,615	327%
28 Churches Represented by Denominational Executives	555	1,468	913	165%	1,681	213	36%
12 Projected Daughter Churches					370		
TOTAL					2,051	583	40%

El Limon, Venezuela
June 5-8, 1972
C. Peter Wagner

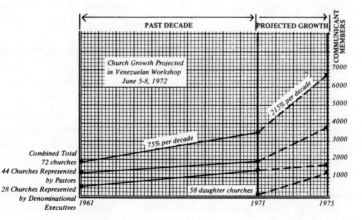

PHASE IV After the projections were made, it became evident that the participants were warming up to learning new methods. At this point class sessions were injected in which methods that God has blessed in the past were analyzed. Sharing what God has done through others in their own particular areas as well as around the world through specific methods brought new challenge and vision to each one. Here is where recommended reading and studies in church growth materials were introduced. Books had been stocked previously and were offered for sale as basic texts. The stock of Weld-McGavran's Spanish text, *Principles of Church Growth* was sold out completely in Venezuela!

CYCLE TWO

Now that goals had been set and the workshop concluded, an evaluation procedure was needed to measure the degree of success or failure of both the workshop and the individual projections.

First, within a matter of days a mimeographed report containing the statistical summary and projections of each participating pastor and denominational representative was compiled and sent out to all who attended the workshop. This served both as a reminder of their projections of faith and as a summary analysis of individual and combined reports. One year later these same figures provided the basis upon which a factual evaluation of the evangelistic efforts during the succeeding year were to be measured.

Second, this practical how-to-do-it *Manual for Evangelism/Church Growth* was prepared as a teaching and evaluation tool for future workshops as well as for self-teaching help for other pastors at the grassroots level who are not able to get to the workshop.

Reports of the first workshop in Venezuela struck such an immediate, responsive chord in other countries that we were unable to make even a preliminary evaluation of its effectiveness before requests began to come in and arrangements were made for similar experiments elsewhere. It soon became evident that such an evaluation tool was urgently needed. During the year that ensued, requests for publication of the Manual in other languages came from a dozen or so countries. The Spanish edition was off the press in time for use in the Second Workshop in Venezuela.

Third, the most important innovation in Venezuela was the projection of three annual workshops. The second workshop was held June 25-29, 1973. Sixty-four pastors, missionaries and church leaders enrolled in contrast to 47 the previous year. The Lutherans did not return, but ASIGEO (related to Orinoco River Mission), ADIEL (Evangelical Free Church), OVICE (related to the Evangelical Alliance Mission), Foursquare and United World Mission workers came back with progress reports. Joining them for the first time were World Evangelization Crusade, Presbyterian and independent workers.

The reports from those who returned showed that church growth principles really work. Some of the stories of effective evangelism told by those who were motivated by the first workshop are remarkable.

The following chart summarizes the progress reports of those who came back the second time. All percentages are *decadal* rates of growth, i.e. the growth of the church over a ten-year period, based on the imprecise, but helpful device of multiplying one year's growth rate by ten or five year's rate by two, etc.

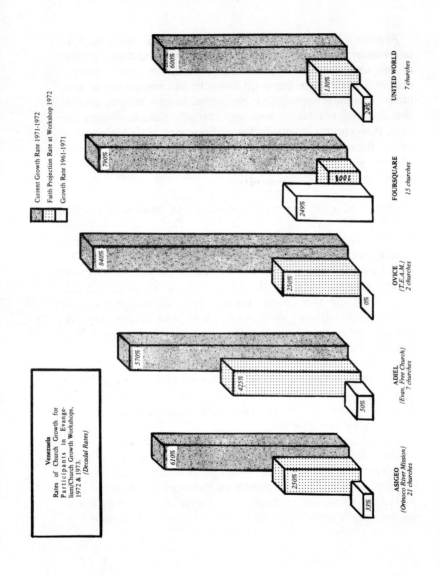

Venezuela
Rates of Church Growth for Participants in Evangelism/Church Growth Workshops, 1972 & 1973.
(Decadal Rates)

Current Growth Rate 1971-1972
Faith Projection Rate at Workshop 1972
Growth Rate 1961-1971

ASIGEO
(Orinoco River Mission)
21 churches
610%
250%
33%

ADIEL
(Evan. Free Church)
7 churches
570%
425%
50%

OVICE
(T.E.A.M.)
2 churches
840%
250%
0%

FOURSQUARE
15 churches
790%
1100%
249%

UNITED WORLD
7 churches
600%
130%
24%

Growth rates in themselves do not tell the whole story. You must be aware of the statistics behind them in order to evaluate the situation properly. The following chart translates the rates to actual numerical growth. The Difference in percentages from the chart on page 35 is due to the fact that some churches represented in the first workshop did not return, so that we were dealing with a slightly different set of churches.

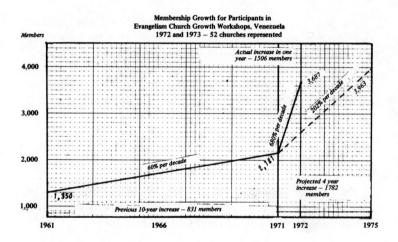

Membership Growth for Participants in
Evangelism Church Growth Workshops, Venezuela
1972 and 1973 — 52 churches represented

Scientifically, of course, even these figures do not necessarily prove that there was a cause and effect relationship between learning the principles of church growth and effectiveness in making disciples. The change from 60% decadal growth to 680% decadal growth could be just a coincidence. But the participants themselves attributed the dramatic upsurge to the new outlook they had acquired and the new principles they had learned. The principles of goal-setting and evaluation, the resistence-receptivity of peoples, and the multiplication of daughter churches were most frequently mentioned as especially helpful.

It is not the purpose of these workshops to offer the participants a "canned" approach to evangelism. Instead models are presented along with theoretical considerations so that they can see how God is working in other places. The second year Venezuela itself provided many new models. But the participants are carefully instructed not to attempt to duplicate any successful program of evangelism in their own local situation. Rather they are to use their own methods, incorporating with them useful ideas that emerge from the other models.

As those who returned the second time shared what God had been doing during the year, they discovered that their combined goals for five years had almost been realized in one year! The 52 churches representing the 7 mission groups participating reported 3,687 new members during the year! One of the groups (related to the Orinoco River Mission) had rather timidly trusted God for 14 new churches a year ago. At the second workshop they joyously reported 19 new churches in *one* year rather than in *four* as they had projected. Their goal now: 24 more by 1977.

All of the participants were even more optimistic as they looked to the future in prayer and faith. Here is what the new projections for the *SECOND CYCLE* looked like:

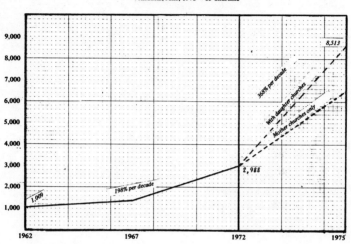

**Faith Projections Made in
Second Annual Evangelism/Church Growth Workshop,
Venezuela, June, 1973 — 65 Churches**

CYCLE THREE

The full impact and long-range value will depend upon a continuing evaluation procedure on an annual basis. Statistics and graphs are never an end in themselves. But they do provide the bedrock data for measuring the quality of evangelistic efforts and, to a significant degree, the health of churches.

SECTION III

AIDS FOR DIAGNOSING YOUR EVANGELISTIC PROGRAM

AIDS FOR DIAGNOSTIC RESEARCH

Research is the means by which your family doctor can diagnose the health of your body. He knows that each organ in the body has a specific function. He also knows that its function is measured in terms of its purpose or goal. He can tell whether an organ of the body is functioning properly. And whether the body as a whole is fulfilling its ultimate purpose or goal. This is done through careful statistical research. He calls it diagnostic research.

To aid him the doctor has at his fingertips various kinds of charts, graphs, statistical instruments and apparatus for measuring function. The thermometer measures the temperature of the patient in exact figures. The stop watch helps the nurse accurately count the number of pulse beats per minute. An electrocardiogram traces the activity of the heart on a graph. The test tube measures the amount of sugar in the blood stream. The scales in the doctor's office enable him to compare your weight with that of a month or a year ago. On the walls of his office and on his desk are many kinds of charts and graphs and statistics.

The doctor is constantly recording numerical data and comparing one set of figures with another. He graphs out your physical progress. He notes significant changes in its pattern and course. All of these aids help him to make an accurate diagnosis of your health. They are all *quantitative* measurements. On the basis of his *quantitative* research, he is able to make a *qualitative* judgment as to how well the members of your body are functioning in terms of their overall purpose.

I Cor. 12:12-29   Eph. 4:4-16   Rom. 12:4-5

The church is the body of Christ. It has many members. Each has its particular function. Both individually and collectively these members fulfill the overall evangelistic purpose or goal of "making disciples", i.e. responsible, reproducing Christians and responsible, reproducing churches. To each member is given one or more specific, spiritual gifts to aid him in the fulfillment of his God-given function.

Research is a means by which you can diagnose the health of your church or churches. Every member functions in cooperation with other members in order to fulfill the overall goal of evangelism/church growth. Since function can be measured in terms of this purpose or goal, you can know whether individually and/or collectively the members of the body are fulfilling their function. This is done through careful statistical research.

To aid you are various kinds of charts, graphs, statistical instruments and apparatus for measuring the functions of the body of Christ. To be sure, these aids are not nearly as well developed or refined as those in the medical profession. They are not nearly as accurate as the doctor's proven instruments. The science of diagnostic research in evangelism/church growth is still in an experimental stage. But here are some practical, how-to-do-it steps to follow with examples of statistical aids which can help you:

Step 1

COMPILE MEMBERSHIP STATISTICS
FOR THE PAST 10 YEARS

Church membership statistics provide the bedrock of data necessary for diagnosing the health of your church. Better than anything else, membership statistics quantify the quality of your church. We could argue about definitions of membership, and definitions are important, but for the time being use whatever you and the leaders of your particular church think is the best definition. Just be consistent — don't use one definition one year and another the next year. Most churches find that counting the active, communicant members gives the best results. Sunday school attendance, church attendance, children of believers, sympathizers, and other such groups are not as good for diagnosis as church membership.

Some churches keep better records than others. If your church does not have good records, do not despair. The job is harder and less accurate, but nevertheless worthwhile. Interview members of your church, asking enough questions so that you can make a good guess as to the annual membership statistics. An educated guess for each year is better than no statistics at all.

Construct and fill in a chart like this:

Years	-10	-9	-8	-7	-6	-5	-4	-3	-2	last year	this year
Membership											

Step 2

PLOT THESE STATISTICS ON A GRAPH

A graph gives you a visual picture of what your church has been doing for the past ten years. Rows of figures don't mean too much until you get them on graph paper. Once the picture is drawn you can begin to ask the right questions and do a much better job of diagnosis.

Graphs are not complicated. You can draw one if you follow these simple steps:

A. Fill in the membership chart. Here is an example which we will call simply "The Church in the Valley."

The Church in the Valley
Membership 1962-1972

Years	-10	-9	-8	-7	-6	-5	-4	-3	-2	last year	this year
Membership	160	200	200	140	240	260	300	260	260	280	300

B. Set your scales. The *vertical scale* will indicate your membership, and it needs careful attention to make sure it is uniform. Every division from the bottom up needs to represent the same number of members, although the total is very flexible, depending on the size of your church and your graph paper. Do this on the left hand side of your graph, starting from the bottom which is usually zero. Here are some examples of different scales on the same graph paper:

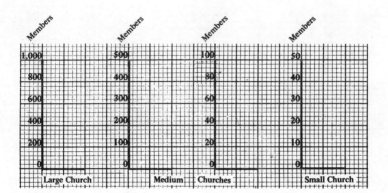

The *horizontal scale*, along the bottom of the graph, is less complicated, since years do not vary. Decide on your spacing for a ten year period, and fill in the years, keeping the distance between each year uniform like this:

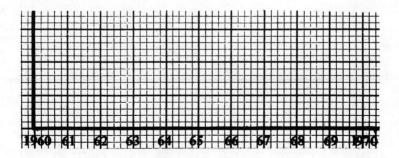

C. Place a dot on the graph for each year according to the membership statistics. Use a pencil so you can erase easily, because mistakes will be made at first. Here is what the Church in the Valley would look like with dots only:

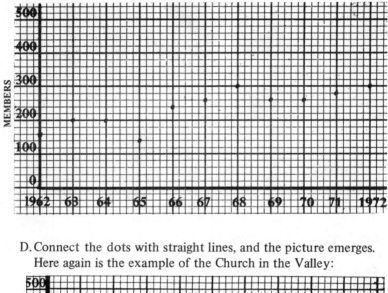

D. Connect the dots with straight lines, and the picture emerges. Here again is the example of the Church in the Valley:

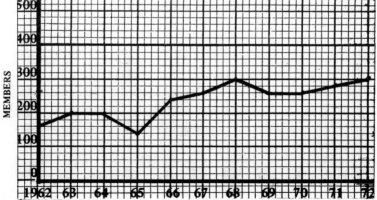

Step 3

CALCULATE THE GROWTH RATES OF YOUR CHURCH

First of all, calculate the rate at which your church grew over the past ten years. This is called the *decadal growth rate*. Here are some examples as to how it is done:

A. Current membership   200
    Membership 10 years ago   − 100
           10 years increase   100

From 100 the church grew by 100 more: rate is 100% per decade.

B. Current membership   500
    10 years ago   − 400
           10 year increase   100

From 400, the church grew by 100 more:
$$\frac{100}{400} = 25\% \text{ per decade}$$

C. Current membership   300
    10 years ago   450
           10 year *loss*   150

From 450, the church *lost* members:
$$\frac{150}{450} = 33\% \text{ } loss \text{ per decade}$$

The decadal rate gives you the over all picture, but from there is is helpful to calculate the rate of increase or decrease for each year. This will reveal some very interesting things about the health of your church that even a graph may not indicate. Let's call this example the "Church on the Hill", and take it for a five year period:

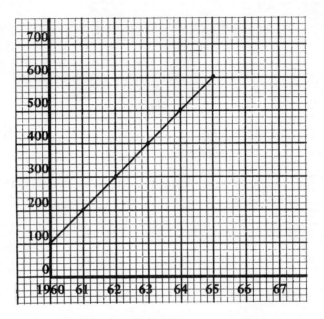

A beginner who looks at this graph might think that the Church on the Hill is a very healthy church. The line goes up rapidly, and it is adding 100 new members per year. But when you calculate *growth* rates for each year, you get a different picture. Notice for example the following:

        1960-61 from 100 it gained 100 members = 100%
        1961-62 from 200 it gained 100 members = 50%
        1962-63 from 300 it gained 100 members = 33%
        1963-64 from 400 it gained 100 members = 25%
        1964-65 from 500 it gained 100 members = 20%

If you plot these rates on a bar graph, you find that your church is *declining* in rate of growth even if membership might be increasing. A church that looks like this is not too healthy, since one of our biblical goals is responsible reproducing Christians, and fewer Christians in this church are reproducing each year:

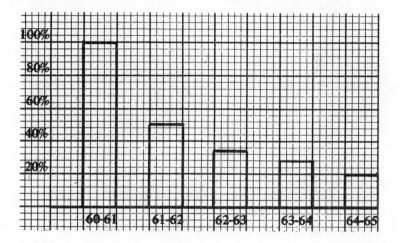

Another way to do this is to plot the same points on a special kind of graph paper called *semi-logarithmic* paper. You will probably only find this in an engineering supply house. There are a few pages in the workbook section of this manual. No need to enter into the mathematical complexities of how this paper is constructed. Suffice it to say that in many cases it helps diagnosis because it shows *rates,* not just numbers in pictorial form. This is easily seen if you compare the following semi-logarithmic graph with the simple linear graph of the

Church on the Hill. Here you can see that the curve is falling off, and in this sense it is not growing at as healthy a rate as you might have suspected from the former graph.

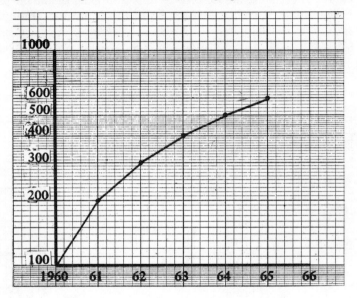

Step 4

COMPARE YOUR GROWTH
WITH THE PROJECTION OF BIOLOGICAL GROWTH

As a rule of thumb, it has been found helpful to project a biological growth rate of 25% per decade for churches across the board. This term "biological growth" does not have any theological implications. Biblically "God has no grandchildren!" But children brought up in committed Christian homes usually accept Christ and join the church when they are old enough, and research has shown that this rate can be calculated at 25% per decade.

This means that if your church is growing at the rate of only 25% per decade, it is not making much progress at all. In order to see this, plot a biological growth line on the graph next to the membership growth line of your church. In order to do this, take the membership during your first year, find 25% (one-fourth) of it, add the two, and plot the total on your final year.

Here is an example of the "Church on the Seashore":

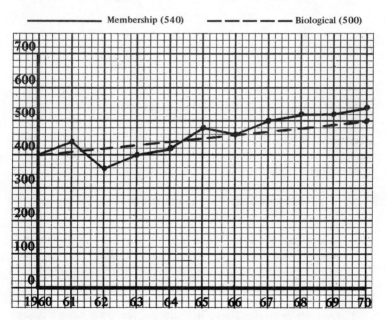

Without the biological growth line, this graph doesn't look bad. But with it, the painful fact becomes obvious that the Church on the Seashore, although it added 140 members in ten years, is not really very healthy. By biological growth alone, it should have reached 500 members, and only 40 others were added through other kinds of growth.

Here is how its biological growth was calculated:

Membership in 1960   400
25% of 400   =   100
                      500 — total membership expected
                             in 1970 through biological
                             growth.

Step 5

REFINE YOUR DATA

We are now getting into more advanced areas of diagnosis, but further refinement is possible if you can find the statistics necessary. If not, let this be a lesson, and plan to gather such statistics for your church in the future. In the meantime, take some educated guesses for the past ten years.

New members are added to the church in three basic ways:

* *Conversion growth.* These are people who, through the ministry of what we have been calling "responsible reproducing Christians" in your church are converted from the world and brought into the church community.

* *Transfer growth.* These include people who have already been converted, are often members of another church, and who join the church by letter of transfer or some other way. But when they first heard of your church, they were already believers.

* *Biological growth.* This has already been explained as including children brought up in homes of believers, and who become members of the church after their conversion.

When all is said and done, the kind of church growth that really exhibits the fruits of effective evangelism is conversion growth. A large percentage of new members every year should fall into this category if your church is healthy.

But the yearly membership figures show net growth, by which we mean the number of new church members *minus* the number of those who leave the church. Generally speaking, people leave for one of three reasons:

* *Reversion or excommunication.* In almost all churches a certain number of once-committed Christians backslide and return to the world. This is the opposite of conversion growth.

* *Transfer out.* These are the members who leave because they move away, or sometimes because they like another church better than yours.

* *Death.* This is the opposite of biological growth.

Very few churches keep statistics that can be plotted to show these refinements graphically, but some do, and diagnosis of the health of such churches is ever so much more meaningful. Here is the way it can be charted in, say, the Church on the River:

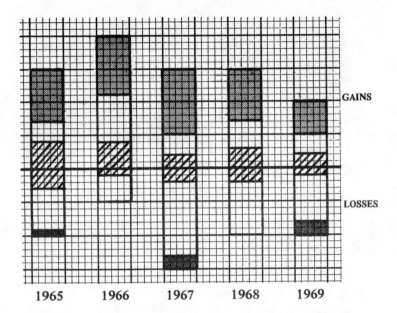

GAINS

LOSSES

1965   1966   1967   1968   1969

KEY

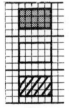

Conversion or Reversion

Transfer in or Out

Biological Growth or Death

1 Square = 5 Members

This kind of analysis tells you much more about the Church on the River than an ordinary graph would. Notice how the linear graph of this church would look:

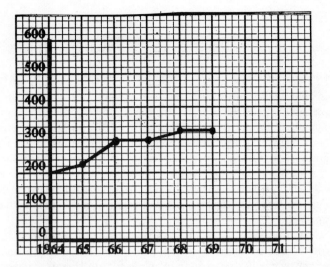

This linear graph tells you a great deal. For instance, the church grew from 200 members in 1964 to 325 in 1969, an increase of 125 members or over 100% per decade. This looks like a healthy church, and it may be. But the bar graph forces you to ask one hard question: why did 180 people transfer out of the church in 5 years? There were 200 members added by conversion growth alone over the five years, but the net membership increase was only 125. What happened to the other 75?

The fact that 180 transferred out is not necessarily a sign of poor church health. Maybe they are being used to start new daughter churches in other parts of the city. But on the other hand, maybe they are leaving because they don't like the worship services or because the believers are continually squabbling among themselves, or for some other reason like that. The point is that a responsible church leader must find the answer to this question if he is going to do the best job possible. Without the bar graph the question might never even have come up.

Step 6

ANALYZE YOUR CHURCH'S GROWTH PATTERNS

This is the last step in diagnosis. If you have done your research well, following steps 1-5 as carefully as possible, by now you should be able to ask the important questions about your church's present state of health. The question in Step 5 about transfers out of the church is an example. One good thing about that Church on the River is the large number of conversions each year. Their evangelistic program is working well, and probably should be continued, although something might be wrong with the pastoral care of believers that could be improved.

One hundred churches analyzed in this manner would produce one hundred different sets of questions. Therefore, no one pattern will suffice as an example for all. Here is the picture of a church in Korea, which needs a good deal of analysis before the truth is known:

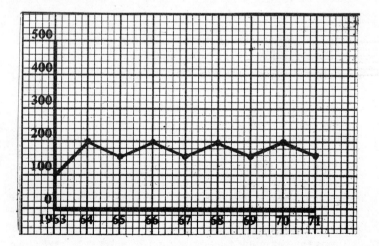

The first question this graph raises is: why can't this church grow? It adds 50 members every other year, then loses them again. The answer is that it is a mother church, continually planting daughter churches. Every other year a group of families leaves the church in order to start a new church. Since their church building only seats 200 people comfortably, they feel this is their optimum growth, and they reproduce on a regular basis. This is not an unhealthy church. It is a "responsible, reproducing church." An additional graph needs to be drawn, with a second line reflecting not only the membership of the mother church, but combining the mother with her spiritual daughters. It might look like this:

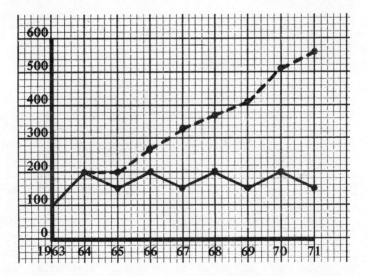

The broken line is the "family growth" of this mother church, and it is the line that in terms of the fulfillment of the Great Commission really counts most. It is a healthy church, responsible and reproducing.

At this point it is necessary to make some comparisons with the growth patterns of other churches. Plot them on the same graph if you can. This is the advantage of having several pastors of your area and/or your denomination in the same evangelism/church growth workshop, using the same manual, talking with the same vocabulary, and coming up with research that lends itself to comparison. It goes without saying that if other churches more or less like yours, even if they are not in the same denomination, are growing rapidly while yours is barely holding its own, something is wrong and needs correction. Nothing substitutes for careful, comparative studies.

Spend as much time as is needed on Step 6. When it is done, you have concluded your diagnostic research, and you are now ready to set goals for future church growth.

SETTING THE GOALS

On the basis of the research and analysis done, you can now set goals for the future growth of your church. These goals should be set in terms of obedience to Christ's Great Commission as we have pointed out in earlier sections. Keep these points in mind:

* *Goals must be set in prayer.* This must not be carnal, but spiritual. As you pray, God will guide you in setting the goals that will please Him.

* *Goals must be set in faith.* When you project membership goals, you are asking the question: "How many new disciples can I trust God to make through me and my church over the next five years?"

* *Goals must be realistic.* Christian goals must not be pipe dreams, reflecting only wishful thinking. You know your area, you know what has been done in the past, you know

the strong and weak points of your congregation, and on the basis of all these things, you must project your goals. Now, here is how to do it:

1. Follow the six steps above, accurately diagnosing the health of your church.

2. Take a new piece of graph paper, plot the past five years growth, and then leave room for five years into the future. Here's what it looks like for the Church in the Valley (Step 2):

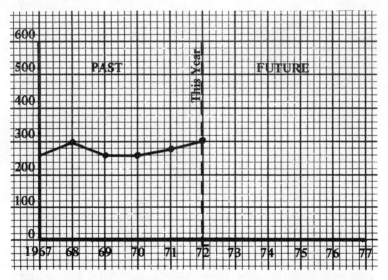

Next, take the current membership and plot a dotted line for the next five years of biological growth. In this case, the current membership is 300. Biologically, this church should grow 25% or by 75 new members over the next *ten* years. But we are projecting only five years, therefore we take half, or 37 new members. In other words by biological growth it should grow from 300 to 337 members by 1977. The graph looks like this:

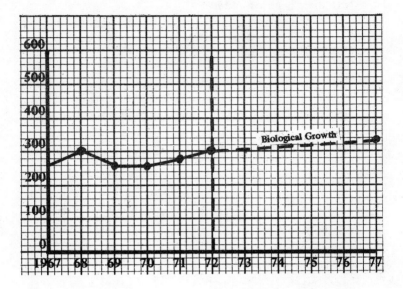

The biological point should be the starting point for your own goal-setting. In other words, if your church grows only to the biological point, it is not really growing at all in terms of winning people from the world to Christ. How many more can you trust God for over the coming years? After prayer and consultation, plot a point and draw a line. The Church in the Valley might project something like 450 members at the end of five years. This would be about 50% growth in five years, not a bad rate. It would look like this:

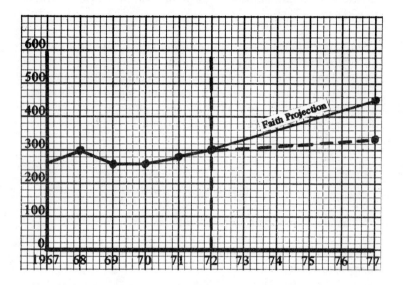

Be sure you do not do this alone. Draw others into the process of setting goals. Your church leaders will become enthusiastic if they are allowed to help. Leaders of other churches in the area will help keep you honest if you have to defend your goals in consultation with them, and especially if they also are setting goals. Mutual comparisons of effectiveness will help.

Evaluating Progress

Just as physicians like to make an annual check up of the health of their patients, you will want to make an annual check up to see whether you are meeting the goals, surpassing them, or falling short. This is easy to do since the line crosses every year at the precise point. For example the Church in the Valley should have 325 members in 1973 and 355 in 1974, according to projections.

At every annual check up, a new five-year graph should be drawn. Adjustments up or down can be made to fit changing circumstances. This procedure should become as much a part of your church life as Sunday morning worship, Christmas programs, or youth meetings. It is necessary if you are going to develop a responsible, reproducing church.

ADDITIONAL RESEARCH

A medical doctor's basic diagnostic research will often lead to further refinement, research and specialization in one or more related areas. With the same careful attention to detail, the medical specialist will analyze, record and compare specific data on, let's say, the function of the kidneys or the symptoms and causes of a particular allergy. All of this is directly related to the general basic research done by your family doctor and contributes to the over all health index.

Statistics and studies on church membership are like the basic diagnostic research of your family doctor. They give the over all health index of the church. But they need not stop there. They are the foundation upon which further research, refinement and specialization can be built. While the workbook section which follows only includes forms and graphs for recording basic membership statistics, there are a vast number of other ways by which you can measure specific areas of your church life and determine your progress or discover your weaknesses. Here are a few areas and suggestions you might want to follow up:

WORSHIP Keep detailed week-by-week records of participation. Graph them not according to members, non-members but regular attendance, and new people. Periodically give yourself a "medical" check up. Compare statistics with membership totals. If attendance is consistently lower than membership figures, something is wrong. Either the membership roll is not accurate and "excess weight" needs to be taken off, or members themselves are not actively and faithfully participating in the worship of your church.

The reverse is also true. If attendance soars far above membership, then something needs to be done to make those who regularly attend responsible church members. Remember that church membership is the basic index for church health. Worship is qualitative, but it can be measured quantitatively. Set realistic goals for worship just as you do for church membership.

PRAYER The Parable of the Harvest concludes with this essential ingredient for a healthy church. Prayer is the dynamic by which the Lord of the Harvest thrusts laborers into His vineyard. It is the key to mobilization and to multiplying church members and congregations. And prayer can be structured. Prayer involvement is measurable. It can be measured by the number of prayer cells or home meetings. It can be measured by the number of people who are praying. It can be graphed according to the mobilization of your membership for prayer. Requests and answers to prayer can be statistically charted. You'd be surprised what a chart on prayer can say to you, or what a lift in spirit a comparison of requests and answers on a chart can give you. Try diagnostic research aids in evaluating the health of your church in terms of prayer. Quantitative analysis will help you assess qualitative prayer.

RENEWAL

Even spiritual renewal can become visually meaningful on a piece of graph paper. What about charting your recent surge in decisions for Christ? Compare with a year ago. You can record growing interest in personal Bible study, intercessory prayer, sharing Christ with others, "each-one-win-one" goals, etc. To be sure, you can't structure the intervention of the Holy Spirit, but you can mobilize to accomplish *His* purposes and chart month-by-month results which *He* has accomplished through the faithfulness of *His* people.

FINANCES

Making responsible church members and responsible churches means making every disciple financially responsible for the on-going of his church. In areas of the world where economy hardly enters into the thinking of the church, this would have less meaning. But in most places, church finances are directly related to Christian and church maturity and hence to the end goal of evangelism/church growth. Statistical planning and analysis could well give a thermometer reading of the evangelistic fervor of your church.

◆

Now that we have the diagnosis we are ready for the prescription. Each church is as individual and distinct as are people. Just as a doctor does not give the same prescription to every individual, so there is no pre-determined pre-fabricated program that will work in every case. Your evangelistic outreach must be prescribed on the basis of your diagnostic research. The following workbook helps you to evaluate your present situation and move on from there to make plans for future growth in faith. You will also be able to run yearly check-ups on your progress by using the workbook.

The methods, or prescription, are up to you, as long as you keep in clear focus the objective of the Great Commission, that of "making disciples," and resulting in responsible, reproducing Christians and responsible, reproducing churches.

Notice that many of those who do not yet know Christ are not within easy reach of your church evangelistic program. This manual is geared primarily to evangelism in "Jerusalem and Judea" to use the terminology of Acts 1:8. Multitudes of other peoples are found across cultural barriers, in "Samaria" and in the "uttermost parts of the earth." The average local church is not set up to win these people to Christ, although it is part of its responsibility to do so. Special Christian organizations, often called missions or orders, throughout history have been used by God for this type of cross-cultural evangelism, but it would take another manual to develop this concept further. It will be more helpful if we stick to "Jerusalem and Judea" while recognizing the equally valid imperative to reach "Samaria and the uttermost parts of the earth."

For further reading:

Donald McGavran, "The Facts Needed," and "Discovering the Why of It," in *Understanding Church Growth* (Grand Rapids, Eerdmans, 1970), pp. 83-122.

Alan R. Tippett, "Problems of Non-Growth," in *Church Growth and the Word of God* (Grand Rapids, Eerdmans, 1970), pp. 47-57.

C. Peter Wagner, "Anticipatory Strategy," in *Frontiers in Missionary Strategy* (Chicago, Moody Press, 1971), pp. 106-121.

SECTION IV

A PERSONAL WORKBOOK
FOR   EVALUATING
EVANGELISTIC
EFFECTIVENESS

A PERSONAL WORKBOOK FOR EVALUATING
EVANGELISTIC EFFECTIVENESS

From this point on, the initiative is yours. If you have taken seriously the contents of the preceding sections, you will want to give much time to using this workbook to evaluate the effectiveness of your own evangelistic work, and then to make whatever changes are necessary to better fulfill the Great Commission.

Notice that the examples given in Steps 1-6 relate to single churches (and their daughters). But this workbook can be used for other situations. For example:

* It can be used for *regional supervisors.* If you are in charge of an area which includes several churches of your denomination, you can combine statistics and evaluate the evangelistic effectiveness of all of them together while the pastors are evaluating their own local churches.

* It can be used by *circuit pastors.* Leaders who are pastoring several churches can combine them statistically, although it is most valuable to do both this, and to do a separate study of each local church.

* It can be used by *denominational executives.* Denominational totals should be studied by this system, although
  again it should supplement local studies, not substitute for
  them.

Remember that these graphs can be set up with any numbers
on the vertical scales, as long as the spacing is kept uniform. In
one person's workbook, a graph might represent a total of 100
members, while in another's it could represent 10,000, depending on the circumstances and on the church or churches being
analyzed.

CHURCH_____YEARS_____

(Steps 1 & 2)

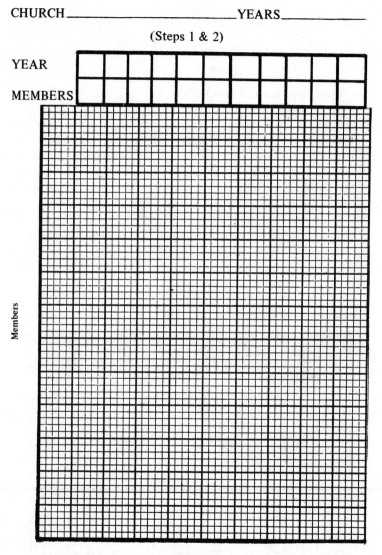

YEAR

MEMBERS

Members

Years

CHURCH_____ YEARS_____

(Step 3)

Calculate your yearly growth rates:

From 19_____ to 19___ , _____ to_____ = _____ %
From_____to_____, _____ to_____ = _____ %
From_____ to_____, _____ to_____ = _____ %
From_____ to_____, _____ to_____ = _____ %
From_____ to_____, _____ to_____ = _____ %
From_____ to_____, _____ to_____ = _____ %
From_____ to_____, _____ to_____ = _____ %
From_____ to_____, _____ to_____ = _____ %
From_____ to_____, _____ to_____ = _____ %
From_____ to_____, _____ to_____ = _____ %

Construct a bar graph:

CHURCH _____ YEAR _____

(Step 3, continued)
Logarithmic graph

Plot your 10-year growth on this semi-logarithmic graph paper (See p. 50)

Members

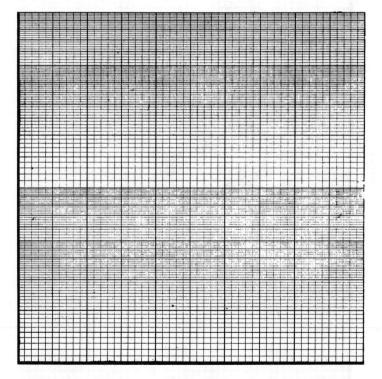

Years

CHURCH_____ YEARS_____

(Step 4)

Comparison with biological growth rate. (See   p. 51)

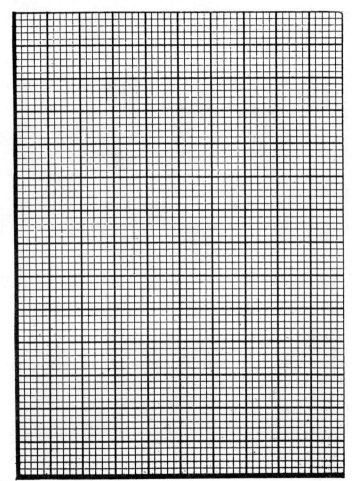

Members

Years

CHURCH_____ YEARS_____

(Step 5)

Plot on a bar graph your pattern of membership gains and losses
(See p. 54)

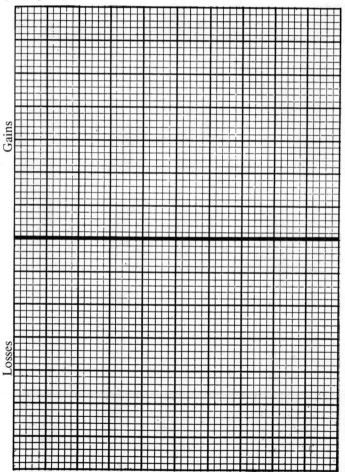

CHURCH_____ YEARS_____

(Step 6)

Compare the growth of your church with other similar churches on this graph:

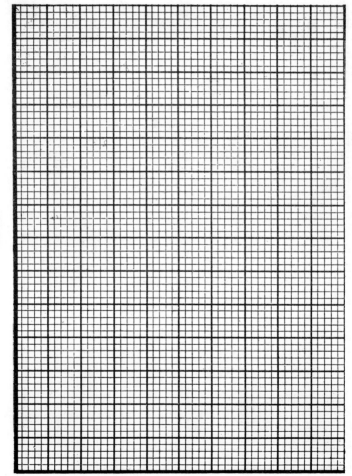

Members

Years

CHURCH _____ YEARS _____

SETTING NEW GOALS
(See pp. 58-61)

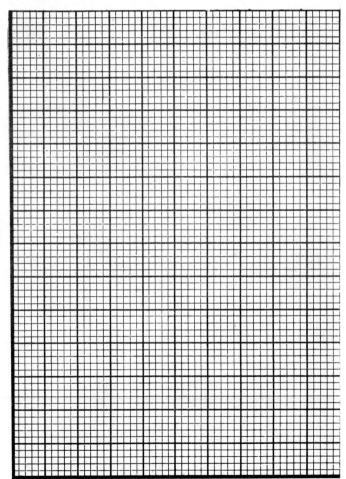

Members (vertical axis label)

Years

FIRST YEAR CHECK UP

NOTES

CHURCH_____YEARS_____

(Steps 1 & 2)

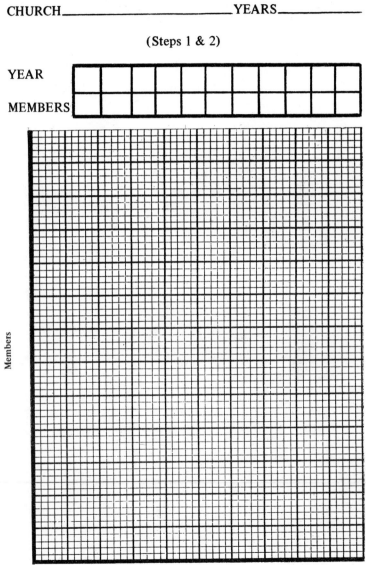

YEAR

MEMBERS

Members

NOTES

CHURCH_____ YEARS_____

(Step 3)

Calculate your yearly growth rates:

From 19_____ to 19_____, _____ to _____ = _____ %
From_____ to _____, _____ to _____ = _____ %
From_____ to _____, _____ to _____ = _____ %
From_____ to _____, _____ to _____ = _____ %
From_____ to _____, _____ to _____ = _____ %
From_____ to _____, _____ to _____ = _____ %
From_____ to _____, _____ to _____ = _____ %
From_____ to _____, _____ to _____ = _____ %
From_____ to _____, _____ to _____ = _____ %
From_____ to _____, _____ to _____ = _____ %

Construct a bar graph:

NOTES

CHURCH _____ YEAR _____

(Step 3, continued)

Logarithmic graph

Plot your 10-year growth on this semi-logarithmic graph paper
(See pp. 50)

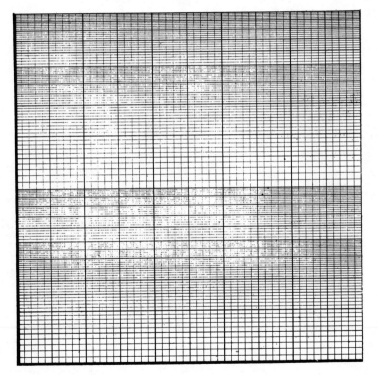

Members

Years

NOTES

CHURCH_____ YEARS_____

(Step 4)

Comparison with biological growth rate. (See   p. 51)

Members

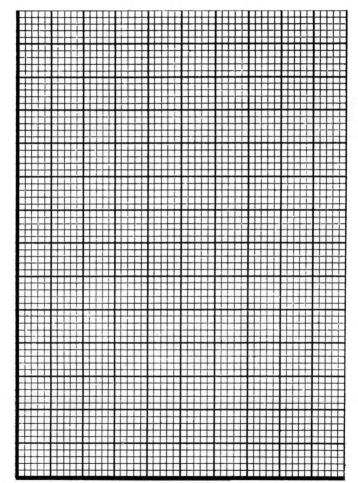

Years

NOTES

CHURCH_____ YEARS_____

(Step 5)

Plot on a bar graph your pattern of membership gains and losses (See   p. 54)

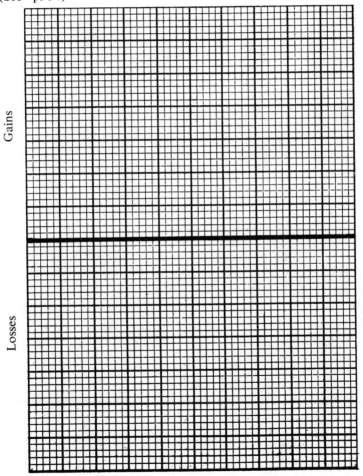

NOTES

CHURCH_____ YEARS _____

(Step 6)

Compare the growth of your church with other similar churches on this graph:

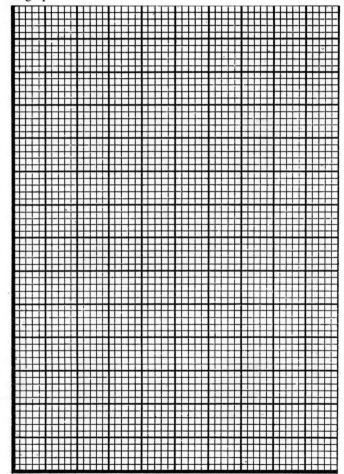

Members

Years

NOTES

CHURCH_____ YEARS_____

SETTING NEW GOALS
(See pp. 58-61)

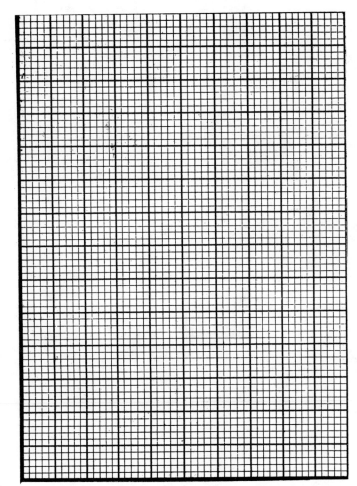

Members

Years